The Skills in English Course Level 1 Part A

Resources Book

Terry Phillips and Anna Phillips

Published by
Garnet Publishing Ltd.
8 Southern Court
South Street
Reading RG1 4QS, UK

© 2006 Garnet Publishing Ltd.

ISBN-13: 978-1-85964-856-8
ISBN-10: 1-85964-856-8

British Library Cataloguing-in-Publication Data
A catalogue record for this book is available from
the British Library.

Production

Project managers:	Maggie Macintyre, Richard Peacock
Editorial team:	John Bates, Emily Clarke, Natalie Griffith, Sarah Margetts, Katharine Mendelsohn, Nicky Platt, Lucy Thompson
Art Director:	David Rose
Design:	Mark Slader
Illustration:	Beehive Illustration (Dave Bowyer/Janos Jantner/Mark Ruffle/Simon Rumble/Roger Wade Walker), Janette Hill, Doug Nash, Karen Rose, Ian West
Photography:	Corbis (Chris Lisle/Stapleton Collection/ Dennis Marsico/Wolfgang Kaehler/ Hulton-Deutsch Collection/Bettman), Digital Vision, Flat Earth, Image Source, Photodisc, Istockphoto

Garnet Publishing wishes to thank the following for their
assistance in the development of this project:
Dr Abdullah Al Khanbashi, Abderrazak Ben Hamida,
Maxine Gillway, Glenys Roberts and the Level 1 team at
UGRU, UAE University.

Printed and bound
in Lebanon by International Press

The Skills in English Course Level 1 Part A

Resources Book

Contents

Advice for New Students

Introduction

First, consider these questions:

1 Are you living away from home for the first time?	If *yes*, read paragraph 1 opposite. ✔
2 Are you sharing a bedroom for the first time?	If *yes*, read paragraph 2 opposite. ✔
3 Is your college work harder than your school work?	If *yes*, read paragraph 3 opposite. ✔
4 Have you made a lot of new friends at college?	If *no*, read paragraph 4 opposite. ✗
5 Do you go to bed early?	If *no*, read paragraph 5 opposite. ✗
6 Do you eat sensibly?	If *no*, read paragraph 5 opposite. ✗
7 Do you understand everything in the classes?	If *no*, read paragraph 6 opposite. ✗

Advice

1 **College life means ... living away from home**
You are responsible for managing your time now. Buy a calendar and mark all the important dates and times on it – the start of the semester, the times of classes, the dates for assignments, the dates of tests.

2 **College life means ... sharing a room**
Perhaps you have your own bedroom at home, but at college you must share a room. You do not have to make friends with your roommate, but you must respect him or her. Always be polite. Always ask before you borrow things from your roommate.

3 **College life means ... working harder**
Don't worry if you find college work hard at first. It is not a problem with you or your intelligence. All first-year students feel the same.

4 **College life means ... making new friends**
You will make new friends at college, but it takes time. Don't worry if you don't have any friends at first. It is not a problem with you or your personality. All first-year students feel the same.

5 **College life means ... taking care of yourself**
You must take care of your health. Get enough sleep. Eat sensibly. Work hard, but relax, too, with sports and leisure activities.

6 **College life means ... having a second chance**
If you don't understand something the first time, you can:
- check it out in the library.
- look it up on the Internet.
- ask the people in your group.
- ask your instructor.
- ask a student advisor.

College Life Is Not Just College Work

You are an adult now. You make your own weekly schedule. But in that schedule, you must make time for four areas of your life.

The four areas are:

- **personal care** – looking after yourself
- **college work** – doing assignments, studying, revising
- **family responsibilities** – keeping in touch, helping family members
- **social life** – enjoying yourself!

Each area of your life is important. Are you neglecting any of the parts? Answer the questions in our check list to find out.

personal care

college work

Your weekly schedule →

family responsibilities

social life

Check list of activities in your weekly schedule

Important area	Do you ...	
personal care	have regular meals?	
	take exercise regularly?	
	get enough sleep?	
college work	do assignments on time?	
	attend all classes?	
	revise for tests?	
social life	meet friends regularly?	
	play sports?	
	relax at the weekend?	
family responsibilities	keep in touch regularly?	
	spend time with the family?	
	deal with family problems?	

College News 28 January Issue 346

Making the Most of Your College Years

Try hard

Play hard

Accept personal responsibility

Set targets

What did your parents say before you left for college? If your parents are like mine, they said: 'Make the most of college. It's the best time of your life.' Perhaps they are right, but how do you make the most of college?

Find a mentor

I asked my students and then I put their ideas together. Here is my four-point FAST way to making the most of your college years.

FIND A MENTOR
That means someone who can tell you what to do. Second-year students know all about the first year. They can tell you how to make the most of it. They can also give you advice about things you shouldn't do.

ACCEPT PERSONAL RESPONSIBILITY
You can make your college years a success. You. Nobody else. Once you accept personal responsibility, you are on the right road.

SET TARGETS
What do you want from your time at college? Decide now and try to reach that target.

TRY HARD, PLAY HARD
Very few people succeed at anything without working hard. Hard work now will give you an easier future. But you can't work hard all the time. Take a break. In fact, take lots of breaks. It is much easier to get back to hard work when you have had a rest.

Get Set
WORK EXPERIENCE COMPANY

We are looking for students for work experience jobs this summer.

The Jobs

There are two types of work experience jobs at Get Set.

5 Firstly, there are holiday jobs in the tourist industry. For example, you can work in a hotel or a restaurant. The jobs are hard but very interesting.

10 Secondly, there are career-entry jobs in many different fields. For example, you can work in teaching, the law or engineering. You get experience in these jobs before you choose a career.

15

Length of Employment

Most holiday jobs last through the summer. They usually start in late June and end in early August. They are full-time.

20 Career-entry jobs are shorter. They usually last for three or four weeks. They are part-time. You work for two or three hours a day.

Requirements

You must have a secondary certificate. You must be in 25 full-time education. You must be 18 for a holiday job. You must be 19 for a career-entry job.

Benefits

You earn between $10 and $15 per hour. You also get free 30 accommodation.

Work Schedule

You work a five-day week in both holiday jobs and career-entry jobs. You usually work from 9 a.m. to 5 p.m. You can do 35 overtime at the weekends and in the evenings in a holiday job. You receive extra money for this work. You cannot do overtime in a career-entry job. 40

Get Set
WORK EXPERIENCE COMPANY

The Work Experience Centre

● Do you want to earn some money this summer?

● Do you want to get useful experience for your future career?

What do we need?

We are looking for young, energetic people. We offer work experience jobs in many fields. We put students in schools, legal offices and police stations to work as teachers, clerks and police cadets.

When do we need you?

Work experience is available for three months in the summer – June, July and August. You can work full time or part time. You can work for the whole of the period or just a few weeks.

What do YOU need?

You must have a secondary certificate. You must be over 19. You must be on a university or college course in the same field as the work experience job. You do not need special skills, but you must be willing to learn 'on the job'.

What do you get?

Full-time workers get the minimum wage. They also get free accommodation and food. Part-time workers get the minimum hourly rate. They do not get accommodation. Both full-time and part-time workers get a completion certificate at the end of the work experience. The certificate gives details of the job and the skills that they have learnt.

When do you work?

Most full-time jobs are 9 to 5. Part-time jobs are sometimes in the morning, and sometimes in the evening. Weekends are free. You will often find the work very hard. But you will learn new skills every day. You will also take an important step towards your chosen career.

5

10

15

20

25

30

Why Is It So Hot?

Table 2:
Average temperature in selected capital cities

Capital cities	Average temperature (in °C)	Line of latitude °N	Distance from the Equator (in km)
Muscat	28.6	23	2,530
Abu Dhabi	27.1	24	2,640
Doha	26.6	25	2,750
Manama	26.1	26	2,860
Kuwait	25.6	29	3,190
Baghdad	22.7	33	3,630
Damascus	17.0	33	3,630

Source: Average temperature information from worldweather.com

WHY ARE SOME PLACES HOTTER than other places? Is there one single factor that affects the average temperature at a location? The simple answer is no.

There are many factors that affect the average temperature. These factors include:

- Is the city surrounded by mountains?
- Is the city on the coast?
- How high is the city above sea-level?

However, there is one main factor that strongly influences the average temperature. That factor is the distance of the city from the Equator. Take Kampala, the capital of Uganda, for instance. It is almost on the Equator, and the average temperature is extremely high, at 29 degrees centigrade.

As you travel north or south from the Equator, the average temperature falls. In Muscat, for example, which is 2,500 kilometres north of the Equator, the average temperature is 28.6. In Damascus, the capital of Syria, which is another 1,100 kilometres north, the average is down to 17.0. So places close to the Equator are generally hotter than places close to the poles. But that still leaves one question.

Why is it so hot at the Equator? It is because the sun is much higher in the sky during the day at the Equator. At the poles, the sun is close to the horizon, so less heat reaches the ground.

5

10

15

20

25

Why Is It Still Dark?

Table 3:
Sunrise on July 1st in selected capital cities

Capital cities	Sunrise on July 1st	Line of longitude °E	Distance from Greenwich longitude (in km)
Muscat	5.22	59	6,490
Abu Dhabi	5.40	54	5,940
Doha	5.46	52	5,610
Manama	5.48	51	5,720
Kuwait City	5.53	48	5,280
Baghdad	5.55	45	4,950
Damascus	6.31	36	3,960

Source: Sunrise times from worldtime.com

PEOPLE WHO TRAVEL IN WINTER from the Gulf to London are often surprised that the sun does not rise in London until 7.30 or 8.00. Why does the sun rise at different times in different places?

There are two factors that affect the time of sunrise. The first factor is related to the distance of the place from the Greenwich meridian. A meridian is a line of longitude. The Greenwich meridian, which runs through London, is the 0° line of longitude. The second factor is related to the distance of the place from the Equator.

Let's consider the first factor. The sun rises in the east. This means that, as we travel to the west, we leave the sun behind, so sunrise is later. For example, in Muscat on July 1st, sunrise is at 5.22, whereas in Damascus, sunrise on the same day of the year is at 6.31. This is because Damascus is around 2,500 kilometres closer to Greenwich than Muscat.

What about the second factor? The Earth is tilted slightly towards the sun. So if you travel north from the Equator, you are actually moving closer to the sun. Take Tehran, for example. The capital of Iran is on almost the same line of longitude as Abu Dhabi, but it is 1,400 kilometres north. Sunrise on July 1st is 5.25 – a quarter of an hour earlier than in Abu Dhabi.

Saudi Arabia – A Brief Introduction

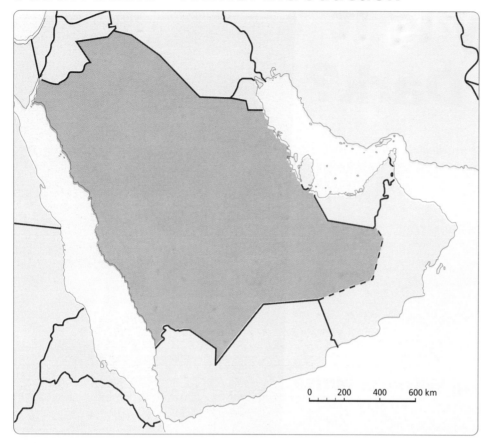

Location	**Saudi Arabia is a large country situated in the region called the Middle East.** It occupies the majority of the Arabian peninsula. It is located between latitudes 16° and 32° North and longitudes 35° and 55° East.
Capital and other main cities	**The capital is Riyadh.** The city is located in the centre of the country. There is another large city, Jeddah, on the Red Sea. It is southwest of Riyadh. 5 Just over 70 kilometres inland from Jeddah is the holy city of Makkah.
Area and borders	**The country covers an area of nearly 2 million square kilometres.** In the west, the country has a long coastline on the Red Sea. To the south, it is bordered by Yemen and Oman. The countries of the United Arab Emirates and Qatar are to the east. There is also a long coastline on the Gulf. To the north, 10 the country is bordered by Jordan, Iraq and Kuwait.
Landscape	**There are mountains along the coast in the west of the country.** The highest point of these mountains is Jebel Sawda, in the southwest corner of the country. It reaches a height of 3,133 metres. There are two large sand deserts. In the north there is the An Nafud and in the south the enormous Rub al Khali desert. 15 The land slopes down to the Gulf in the east. On the eastern coast, there are swamps and salt marshes. There are no permanent rivers in the country. Fresh water comes from oases, wells and wadis.

Bahrain – A Brief Introduction

Location

Bahrain occupies 33 islands in the Gulf. The largest island is also called Bahrain. It lies on latitude 26° North and longitude 50° East. It is situated 20 kilometres east of the coast of Saudi Arabia and 45 kilometres west of Qatar.

Capital and other main cities

5

The capital, Manama, is located on the north coast of Bahrain island. There are no other large cities.

Area

The country has an area of 665 square kilometres. However, the land area is growing because the government is reclaiming land from the sea.

Borders

10

To the south and west is the Gulf of Bahrain. To the north and east is the Gulf. Bahrain has no land borders, but there is a causeway. This connects Bahrain and Saudi Arabia. There are plans for another causeway to link Bahrain and Qatar.

Physical features

The majority of the land is stony or sandy desert. Jebel ad Dukhan is the highest point on the island, but it 15 is only 122 metres high. There are no permanent rivers on any of the islands. Fresh water comes from wells.

Read the sentences. Circle the correct word in each case.

1	She is⟩ / She	French.	
2	She	is / are	single.
3	He	is not / has not	18.
4	Alan	is	teacher. / a teacher.
5	Are you / You are	Lebanese?	
6	Where	are you / you are	from?
7	They	is / are	students.
8	He is	to / at	Greenhill College.
9	I	have / am have	one brother.
10	You do / Do you	have	brothers or sisters?
11	We	likes / like	Maths.
12	Lessons	begin / beginning	at 9.00.
13	Does / Do	lessons end	at 4.00?
14	The course	end / ends	in July.
15	When	begins the course? / does the course begin?	
16	Pierre	reads / is reading	a book at the moment.
17	Is she	share / sharing	with a friend?
18	Where	do / are	you living at the moment?
19	He	loves	to read. / reading.
20	College life means	live / living	away from home.

A Look at all the tables.

1 What colour is each part of speech?
- noun
- adjective
- pronoun
- preposition
- verb

2 What kind of word...
- can be the subject?
- can come after the verb *be*
- can come after other verbs?

B Complete each table.

C Look at Tables 1 and 2.

1 Where can you put *not* in each table?

2 How can you make a question with the answer *Yes* or *No*?

3 How can you make a question with a question word (*What*, *Where*, etc.)?

D Look at Table 3. Tick the correct rule for making negative sentences.

___ Add *not* after the verb.

___ Add *not* before the verb.

___ Add *do not* before the verb.

___ Add *does not* after the verb.

E Write a rule for making negative sentences in Table 4.

F Look at Tables 3 and 4 again. Tick the correct questions.

___ Do they love History?

___ Do you has three sisters?

___ Does lessons begin at 9.00 a.m.?

___ Does the course end in June?

___ You do study Chemistry?

G Compare Tables 1 and 5.
In Table 5, how do you make...
- negative sentences?
- questions?

H Compare Tables 5 and 6.

1 Which words are similar?

2 What part of speech are the *~ing* words in each table?

Table 1: *Pronoun + verb (be) + adj/noun*

Pronoun	Verb	Adjective/noun
I		Jordanian.
You	are	married.
	is	16.
She		a teacher.
	are	students.

Table 2: *Pronoun + verb (be) + prep + noun*

Pronoun	Verb	Prep	Noun
I		from	China.
You	are		Greenhill College.
	is	in	the Arts Faculty.

Table 3: *Pronoun + verb + noun*

Pronoun	Verb	Noun
I		three brothers.
You		Biology.
We		two sisters.
They		Maths.

Table 4: *Pronoun/noun + verb + prep + noun*

Subject	Verb	Prep	Noun
She		for	a bank.
He		to	Greenhill College.
The lesson		at	8.00 a.m.
The course		in	July.

Table 5: *Pronoun + aux (be) + present participle + other information*

S	Verb		Other
I	am		at Greenhill College.
He	is		Chemistry.
She	is		lunch at the moment.
They	are		football at the moment.

Table 6: *Pronoun + verb + gerund + other*

Subject	Verb	Object	Other
College life	means		away from home.
			a room.
			harder.

Read the sentences. Circle the correct word in each case.

1	He is	from	Chinese. (China.)
2	Are you You are	at college?	
3	Marion	is	doctor. a doctor.
4	You do Do you	go to	Greenhill College?
5	When	begins the lesson? does the lesson begin?	
6	Françoise	does is	watching TV at the moment.
7	I	am having have	two sisters.
8	Take you Take	lots of	breaks.
9	Eat not Don't eat	junk food.	
10	Always accept Accept always	responsibility	for your work.
11	Go to bed late never. Never go to bed late.		
12	I	never am am never	late.
13	He	plays sports often. often plays sports.	
14	They	eat in the restaurant often. often eat in the restaurant.	
15	I	every day pray. pray every day.	
16	We study	every afternoon in the library. in the library every afternoon.	
17	I eat in a restaurant	one time once	a week.
18	She writes to her parents	every	weeks. week.
19	How	usually often	do you study at the weekend?
20	What	you do you	do in the evenings?

A Look at all the tables.

  1 What kind of verb doesn't need a subject?

  2 Which of these sentence patterns are possible?
- adjective + verb
- pronoun + adjective + verb
- pronoun + verb + adjective
- pronoun + verb + noun
- pronoun + verb + preposition + other information
- verb + adjective

B Complete each table.

C Look at Table 1.

  1 How do you make this sentence pattern negative?

  2 Where do you put the negative word(s) – position 1, 2 or 3?

  3 Where do you put the frequency adverbs *always*/*never* – position 1, 2 or 3?

D Look at Tables 2, 3 and 4.

  1 Where do you put the frequency adverbs *always*/*usually*/*often*/*never*?

  2 What about *sometimes*?

E There is one mistake in each of these frequency phrases. Find it and correct it.

  1 every days

  2 most day

  3 one time a week

  4 twice week

  5 three time a week

  6 every then and now

F Look again at Tables 2, 3 and 4. Where can you put the frequency phrases in Exercise E?

G Look at Table 5 for one minute. Then close this book and draw the table in your notebook.

Table 1: *Imperative + noun*

1	Verb	2	Noun	3
	Accept		responsibility.	
	Set		targets.	
			friends.	
			breaks.	
			junk food.	

Table 2: *Pronoun + verb + adjective*

1	Pronoun	2	Verb	3	Adjective	4
	I				late.	
	You				tired.	
	He				ill.	
	She		is			
	They		are			

Table 3: *Pronoun + verb + noun*

1	S	2	V	3	O	4		5
			visit				at the weekend.	
			meet				on Fridays.	
	I				college work		in the afternoon.	
			play		sports			

Table 4: *Pronoun + verb + prep + other*

1	S	2	V	3	Prep	4	Other	5
					in		a restaurant.	
							the library.	
	I		go				pray.	
			listen					
			write				my parents.	

Table 5: *Question words + aux + pron + verb + noun*

Question words	Aux	Pron	Verb	Noun
How			visit	your parents?
When	do	you	do	
				at the weekend?

Read the sentences. Circle the correct word in each case.

1	There	is (are)	four types of job.
2	The works here The work here	is	very interesting.
3	Career-entry applicants	do not need	the experience. experience.
4	How long	do they they	want us for?
5	What	need they? do they need?	
6	You	must be must	at least 18.
7	She must	complete completes	the form.
8	They can	working work	overtime if they want.
9	Most of Most	people	work for three months.
10	It is	very a very	hard work.
11	We	need to find an energetic	young. young person.
12	We all work a	five-day five-days	week.
13	We get up early	and but	we go to bed late.
14	The work is very hard	but and	it is very interesting.
15	You can work for one, two	and or	three months.
16	I'm good at English,	so because	I can help teach it.
17	He did not get the job	because so	he was too young.
18	They are looking	for after	new assistants to help them.
19	I would like to work	in at	the weekend.
20	Most holiday jobs last	in from	June to August.

(A) Look at Table 1a.

1 Use these nouns to make statements about a work experience company.

> helpline   website   holiday jobs
> part-time jobs

2 Make *yes/no* questions. (Use *any, many.*)

3 Make the sentences negative. (Use *any, many.*)

4 Add these adjectives to your sentences. Say them to yourself: *useful, short, interesting, friendly*

(B) Look at your work in A and at Table 1b.

1 Write your A4 sentences into **first mention** boxes.

2 How do **first mention** sentences begin?

3 How do **further information** sentences begin?

4 Complete the **further information** sentences.

(C) Look at Table 2.

1 Add *a* and *the* where necessary. If no article is necessary, write nothing.

2 Match a–c and i–iii to form the correct rules.

  a Use *a/an/some* + noun when you …

  b Use *the* + noun when you …

  c Use zero article when you …

    i … refer to all things/people in a group.

    ii … refer to particular things/people we know about.

    iii … first mention particular things/people.

(D) Look at Table 3.

1 Complete the table with these modal verbs:

> must   can   cannot (can't)

2 State rules in your country.

  • To (drive/get married), …

  • If you are not (age), …

(E) Look at Table 4.

1 Circle these prepositions in the time expressions:

> at   during   for   from … to/until
> in   on   through   until

2 Write about your life. Include time expressions.

Table 1a: There + *verb* **(be) +** *noun phrase*

There	Verb	Noun phrase
There	is	a _____
There	is	a _____
There	are	some _____
There	are	a lot of _____

Table 1b: *First mention + further information*

There is/are + first mention	Pronoun + *is/are* + further information
_____ friendly helpline you can call.	_____ open all day.
_____ a useful website.	_____ easy to use.
_____ short part-time jobs.	_____ for three or four weeks.
_____ interesting holiday jobs.	_____ for six weeks.

Table 2: *Indefinite, definite and zero articles*

	Article + noun
Today, we're going to play	_____ game of football.
Well, I don't want to play in	_____ game.
That's because I'm no good at	_____ games.

Table 3: *Modal verbs* **must, can, cannot (can't)**

	Modal verb + verb	
To get a holiday job, you	_____ be	at least 18.
If you work for us, you	_____ get	free accommodation.
If you are not in education, you	_____ work	for us.
To apply for a job, you	_____ complete	a form.

Table 4: *Prepositions in time expressions*

	Time expressions
Zara got the job of counsellor at a summer camp.	(in) April.
Camp started	on June 1.
Now it is early July, so she has been there	for about a month.
She plans to work all the way	through the summer.

Read the sentences. Circle the correct word in each case.

1	A large river runs	(through) along	the city.
2	The sun rises	at in	the east.
3	Tokyo is the capital	of for	Japan.
4	Korea is close	by to	Japan.
5	The Gulf is hot. Doha,	by example, for example,	averages 26.6°C.
6	Bring Take	the Dubai temperature,	for instance.
7	The sun is high at midday,	so because	the temperature rises.
8	Kampala is near the Equator,	whereas however	Muscat is 2,500 km north.
9	People	travel who travel	to London are often surprised.
10	Is there something	that it	causes the temperature to rise?
11	There are two things	which who	affect the temperature.
12	Canada, which is north	of from	the USA is generally cold in winter.
13	Canada is much	coldest colder	than Kuwait.
14	Saudi Arabia is a lot	hotter hoter	than Britain.
15	Driest The driest	month in many countries	is July.
16	In New York, January is the	wetter wettest	month.
17	Sunrise in Doha is at 5.44,	but in Damascus it is an hour	late. later.
18	It was so	cold colder	last night!
19	How high	is the city the city is	above sea level?
20	Why the sun rises Why does the sun rise	at different times	in different places?

A Look at Table 1.

    1 Complete the table with appropriate prepositions of movement. Choose from the following:

across   along   away from   towards   down   up   into   out of   over   under   round   through

    2 Write more pairs of sentences of your own.

Table 1: *Prepositions of movement*

Speakers		Preposition	
Alan	We can't get	_____	the river here.
Peter	But if we walk	_____	the river, we'll find a place.
Nadia	Our plane flew	_____	a storm on the way to Cairo.
Hanan	We didn't come	_____	it until we were nearly there.
Maria	We went	_____	the mountain very slowly.
Rosa	But then we came	_____	again really fast!
Fuad	We need to swim	_____	here. It's dangerous.
Ahmed	Let's move	_____	the beach. It's safe there.

B Many expressions, nouns, adjectives and verbs use particular prepositions. Which prepositions often go with these?

at / for the first time   make friends to / with   responsible about / for the start for / of   take care by / of

C Look at Table 2.

    1 Which comments take each of these forms:
- 1st idea ... 2nd idea that adds (+) to the 1st?
- 1st idea ... 2nd idea that goes against (–) the 1st

    2 Which words introduce (+) ideas?

    3 Which words introduce (–) ideas?

    4 Which words connect 1st and 2nd ideas in one sentence?

    5 Which words start a new sentence for the 2nd idea?

Table 2: *Connectors – additive and contrastive*

1st idea	Connector	2nd idea
Dubai is a big trading centre,	and	it has a large tourist industry.
It has a large port.	In addition,	there is big new airport.
Riyadh is the Saudi capital,	but	Jeddah is the commercial centre.
Jeddah is on the coast,	whereas	Riyadh is in the desert.
Riyadh is the political centre.	However,	Makkah is the religious heart.

D Look at Table 3.

1 Underline the clauses that start with the pronouns *who, which* and *that*.

2 Which of these clauses complete the meaning of the sentence?

3 Which ones add extra information?

4 How do we show that it is extra information? (Think about commas.)

Table 3: *Relative clauses*

	Relative clause	
Egypt is a country	which/that has a long history.	
The Pharaohs were the kings	who/that ruled Ancient Egypt.	
Jordan	, which is west of Iraq,	has several regions.
The Jordanian people	, who live mainly in the north,	have an ancient culture.

E Look at Table 4a. Complete the table with the correct forms of *cold*.

Table 4a: *Comparative and superlative adjectives*

Adjective			
comparative	In winter, Moscow is	_____ _____	any Arab city.
superlative	Vostok, near the South Pole, is	_____ _____	place on Earth.

F Look at Table 4b.

1 Study the spelling rules for comparative and superlative adjectives with:

a one syllable, and **b** two syllables if they end in *y*. Explain the spelling rules in your own words.

2 Give the comparative and superlative forms of these. | close cloudy high nice steep sunny wet |

Table 4b: *Comparative and superlative spellings*

Rules	Adjective	Comparative	Superlative
cold + er/est	cold	_____	_____
dark	_____	_____	_____
large + r/st	_____	_____	_____
late	_____	_____	_____
dry – y + ier/iest	_____	_____	_____
happy	_____	_____	_____
hot + t + er/est	_____	_____	_____
big + g (ending with 1 vowel + 1 consonant)	_____	_____	_____

G Look at Table 5.

1 Complete the questions with these question words. | How far How high What When Where Why |

2 Use the tables on pages 10–11 to answer questions 1–5.

3 Answer question 6 from the first text.

Table 5: *Questions*

Question words	Aux	Noun/pronoun	Verb	Other
_____	does	the sun	rise	in Doha?
_____ time	does	it	rise	in Baghdad?
_____	is	the average temperature		28.6°C?
_____	is	Muscat		from the Equator?
_____	is	the average temperature		in Damascus?
_____	does	Muscat	get	hotter than Damascus?

Read the sentences. Circle the correct word in each case.

1	Oman is to the	eastsouth ~~southeast~~	of Saudi Arabia.
2	Manama is in the	northeastern eastnorthern	part of Bahrain.
3	There is There are	a 26-kilometre causeway	from Bahrain to Saudi Arabia.
4	There is It is	a large desert	in northern Saudi Arabia.
5	There are	no any no	permanent rivers.
6	The highest mountain is	at in	the southwest of Saudi Arabia.
7	Egypt lies	to from	the west of Saudi Arabia.
8	Qatar is east	to of	Saudi Arabia.
9	Jeddah is	in on	the Red Sea coast.
10	Bahrain is	between among	Saudi Arabia and Qatar.
11	Jebel ad Dukhan is in the	central centre	of the island.
12	The majority	of in	the island is desert.
13	Qatar is bordered	by with	Saudi Arabia in the south.
14	Yemen	is are	situated to the south of Saudi Arabia.
15	Qatar and Kuwait	locate are located	on the Gulf.
16	Dubai	is part of	United Arab Emirates. the United Arab Emirates.
17	Bahrain	has is	an area of 665 square kilometres.
18	Jebel Sawda	is	high 3,133 metres. 3,133 metres high.
19	Almost two-thirds of the country	is are	desert.
20	Nine-tens Nine-tenths	of the people	live in cities.

A Look at the compass points.

  1 Work out the other points and add them.

  2 Think of important places and where they are. Make true statements like these.

    • *Makkah is a long way west of here.*

    • *Qatar is a short way northeast of here.*

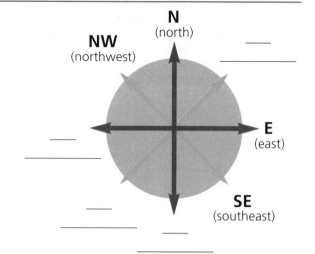

B Look at Table 1.

  1 How do first mention sentences begin?

  2 How do further information sentences begin?

  3 Complete Table 1. (Think: singular or plural?)

Table 1: *There is, There are, It is, They are*

First mention	Further information
_____ a peninsula between the Red Sea and the Gulf.	_____ called the Arabian Peninsula.
In the peninsula, _____ a very large country called Saudi Arabia.	_____ one of the largest of all the Arab countries.
In addition, _____ several small countries in the Peninsula.	_____ all on the coast of the Gulf.
Finally, _____ two medium-sized countries in this region.	_____ Yemen and Oman and they are both south of Saudi Arabia.

C Look at the map of Spain and Table 2.

  1 Use these verbs in their correct forms to complete Table 2.

    cover(s) *lie(s) occupy(ies) is/are bordered *is/are located *is/are situated

  *These verbs all mean roughly the same. Use each one once.

  2 Make similar statements about your country.

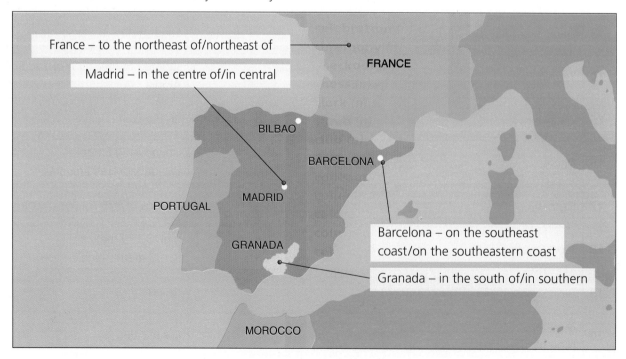

Table 2: *Verbs to express location*

	Verb	
Spain	_____	in the far west of Europe.
This country	_____	the majority of the Iberian Peninsula.
It	_____	an area of about 500,000 square kilometres.
It	_____	by Portugal and France.
The capital, Madrid,	_____	in the middle of Spain.
Morocco	_____	to the south of Spain.

D Look at the map of Spain and Table 3.

1 Complete Table 3 with two phrases for each place.

2 Make similar statements about places in and around your country.

Table 3: *Prepositional phrases to express location*

	Prepositional phrase	
Madrid is	_____	Spain.
France lies	_____	the country.
Granada is situated	_____	Spain.
Barcelona is located	_____	the country.

E Look at Table 4.

1 Complete the table. Use these two patterns.

- *be* (... kilometres long)
- *have a* (length of ... kilometres)

Use this information.

- The River Nile – 6,695 kilometres – long/length
- The Pacific Ocean – *4,000 metres – deep/depth
- The Red Sea – *300 kilometres – wide/width
- Mount Everest – 8,848 metres – high/height

*approximate average

Table 4: *Measurements*

The River Nile	is _____
	_____
	has _____
	_____
The Pacific Ocean	is _____
	_____
	has _____
	_____
The Red Sea	is _____
	_____
	has _____
	_____
Mount Everest	is _____
	_____
	has _____
	_____

F Look at Table 5.

1 Write the words in the table.

a fifth   a quarter   a tenth   a third   four-fifths
seven-tenths   three-quarters   two-thirds

2 Make true statements about things that you know, e.g.:
About a third of my class play football.

Table 5: *Fractions*

$\frac{1}{10}$	_____	$\frac{7}{10}$	_____
_____	_____	_____	_____
$\frac{1}{5}$	_____	$\frac{4}{5}$	_____
$\frac{1}{3}$	_____	$\frac{2}{3}$	_____

Presenter: The Skills in English Course, Level 1 Part A
Theme 1: Education
Section 1: Listening
Lesson 1: Vocabulary for listening
B Listen to some sentences with the green words. Then complete each sentence with one of the words.

Voice: 1 The academic year in my country starts in October. All the students go back to high school then.
2 When does the second semester start? Is it in February?
3 Which room is the lecture in? The one about learning English?
4 Mr Jones is in charge of the library. He is responsible for all the books and CD-ROMs.
5 Who is the head of Year 1? Is it Mrs Wright? Or is she in charge of Year 2?

Presenter: Lesson 2: Practising listening
C It is the start of the college year at Greenhill College. The principal is welcoming the new students. Listen and add the missing information.

Peter Bean: OK. Let's begin. Welcome to Greenhill College. I am very pleased to see you all here.
My name is Peter Bean. I'm the principal – that means I am in charge of the whole place. You come and see me if you have any problems with the fees – that means the money you must pay. My office is on the first floor, Room 15, by the stairs. The people behind me are some of my staff. This is Mrs Polly Penn. She's the head of Year 1. She is responsible for the schedule. After this meeting, Mrs Penn will give you the schedule for the first term. The schedule tells you the times of all your lectures. Mrs Penn will also give you the name of your instructor. We call the teachers at Greenhill instructors. She will also tell you the name of your personal advisor – that's a person who helps you if you have problems. Finally, this is the registrar, Mr Bill Beale. He's in charge of attendance. If you can't come to college one day, tell Mr Beale. OK, that's it from me. Now I'll hand over to Mrs Penn … Oh, I nearly forgot. Mr Beale's room is on the first floor, next to my room – Room 16.

Presenter: E The principal explains the meaning of each word in Exercise D. Listen to his speech again and check your answers.
[REPEAT OF LESSON 2 EXERCISE C]

Presenter: Lesson 3: Learning new listening skills
A Listen and tick the words you hear. If you get three ticks in a line, say Bingo!
[REPEAT OF LESSON 2 EXERCISE C]

Presenter: B 2 Listen and check your answers.
Voice:
pay	– letter p
Bill	– letter b
Penn	– letter p
personal	– letter p
Bean	– letter b
Peter	– letter p
people	– letter p
place	– letter p
pleased	– letter p
Beale	– letter b
Polly	– letter p
principal	– letter p
problems	– letter p
behind	– letter b

Presenter: B 3 Listen to these words connected with education. Is the missing letter p or b?
Voice: a book
b paper
c begin
d spell
e pass
f period
g subject
h explain

Presenter: C 2 Look at these pairs of words. Listen. Which do you hear in each case? Don't worry about the meanings.
Voice: a hill
b steal
c will
d meal
e pill
f kill
g feel
h feet
i Bill
j beat

Presenter: D Listen to the first part of the principal's speech again. It's much slower this time. Put your left hand up every time you hear p. Put your right hand up every time you hear b.

Peter Bean: OK. Let's begin. Welcome to Greenhill College. I am very pleased to see you all here.
My name is Peter Bean. I'm the principal. You come and see me if you have any problems with the fees – that means the money you must pay. My office is on the first floor, Room 15, by the stairs. The people behind me are some of my staff. This is Mrs Polly Penn. She's the head of Year 1. She is responsible for the schedule. After this meeting, Mrs Penn will give you the schedule for the first term. The schedule tells you the times of all your lectures.

Presenter: E Listen to the second part of the speech again. Say i every time you hear the short sound. Say ee every time you hear the long sound.

Peter Bean: Mrs Penn will also give you the name of your instructor. We call the teachers at Greenhill instructors. She will also tell you the name of your personal advisor – that's a person who helps you if you have problems. Finally, this is the registrar, Mr Bill Beale. He's in charge of

Presenter: attendance. If you can't come to the college one day, tell Mr Beale. OK, that's it from me. Now I'll hand over to Mrs Penn … Oh, I nearly forgot. Mr Beale's room is on the first floor, next to my room – Room 16.

Presenter: **Lesson 4: Applying new listening skills**
B Listen to some sentences from the principal's speech in Lesson 2. What is Mrs Penn going to talk about? Tick one or more topics.

Peter Bean: This is Mrs Polly Penn. She's the head of Year 1. She is responsible for the schedule. After this meeting, Mrs Penn will give you the schedule for the first term. The schedule tells you the times of all your lectures. Mrs Penn will also give you the name of your instructor. We call the teachers at Greenhill instructors. She will also tell you the name of your personal advisor – that's a person who helps you if you have problems.

Presenter: **C Listen to Mrs Penn's speech. Underline the topics to check your answers to Exercise B.**

Polly Penn: OK. First, your schedule. In the first term, you do General Studies and English. General Studies means subjects like Religion, Maths, Science and the Arts. So, every day, you do three periods of General Studies in the morning and three of English in the afternoon.
If you have any problems with any of your studies, go and see your personal advisor. The advisors' rooms are on the third floor. Now, listen carefully.
If your surname – I mean your family name – begins with A, B, C, D or E, your advisor is Mrs Piper.
If your surname begins with F, G, H, I or J, your advisor is Mrs Barber.
If your surname begins with K, L, M, N or O, your advisor is Mrs Peebles.
If your surname begins with P, Q, R, S or T, your advisor is Mrs Bream.
If your surname begins with U, V, W, X, Y or Z, your advisor is Mrs Pinner.

Presenter: **D Imagine you are a new student at Greenhill College.**
1 Listen to the first part of Mrs Penn's speech again. Which schedule above is correct for you?

Polly Penn: OK. First, your schedule. In the first term, you do General Studies and English. General Studies means subjects like Religion, Maths, Science and the Arts. So, every day, you do three periods of General Studies in the morning and three of English in the afternoon.

Presenter: **2 Listen to the second part of Mrs Penn's speech again. What is the name of your personal advisor? Tick one.**

Polly Penn: If you have any problems with any of your studies, go and see your personal advisor. The advisors' rooms are on the third floor. Now, listen carefully.
If your surname – I mean your family name – begins with A, B, C, D or E, your advisor is Mrs Piper.
If your surname begins with F, G, H, I or J, your advisor is Mrs Barber.
If your surname begins with K, L, M, N or O, your advisor is Mrs Peebles.
If your surname begins with P, Q, R, S or T, your advisor is Mrs Bream.
If your surname begins with U, V, W, X, Y or Z, your advisor is Mrs Pinner.

Presenter: **Section 2: Speaking**
Lesson 1: Vocabulary for speaking
B Listen and repeat the green words.
Voice: college
meeting
speech
studies
subject
year

Presenter: **Lesson 2: Practising speaking**
B Paula is a first-year student, too. Listen to a conversation between Barbara and Paula. Tick any of your underlined words from the leaflet.
Paula: Hello.
Barbara: Hello, I'm Barbara.
Paula: Hi, I'm Paula.
Barbara: Is this your first day?
Paula: Yes, it is. What about you?
Barbara: Yes, me too.
Paula: What happens today?
Barbara: Well, first there's a speech from the principal.
Paula: What's a principal?
Barbara: The head of a college. He's going to welcome us and introduce the staff.
Paula: What does staff mean?
Barbara: The staff are the people who work at a college.
Paula: Right. Then what?
Barbara: Then there's a meeting with the head of Year 1.
Paula: The head?
Barbara: Yes, the person in charge. She's going to give us the schedule.
Paula: Does schedule mean the subjects and times?
Barbara: That's right. She's also going to tell us the name of our instructor and our personal advisor.
Paula: Is an instructor a teacher?
Barbara: Yes. It's the word for teacher at a college or university.
Paula: What about a personal advisor?
Barbara: It's the person you go to if you have any problems with your studies.
Paula: Ah, I see. How do you know all this?
Barbara: I read the leaflet. Look!

Presenter: **C Listen again. Match each word from the leaflet with its meaning.**
[REPEAT OF LESSON 2 EXERCISE B]

Presenter: **Lesson 3: Learning new speaking skills**
D 2 Listen to Barbara's speech to the tutor group. Make full sentences from Barbara's notes.
Barbara: My name is Barbara Peters.
I'm British.
I'm from Birmingham.
My favourite subject is P.E.
I don't like Biology.

Presenter: **Theme 2: Daily Life**
Lesson 1: Vocabulary for listening
C Listen to some sentences with the green words. Number the words in order.
Voice: 1 There is a very good restaurant in North Road. The food is excellent.
2 I don't like chess. In fact, I don't like any games like that.
3 Do you play any sports? Football, basketball, handball?

4 My sister is excellent at music. She plays the piano, the flute and the guitar.

5 Have you joined the college computer club yet?

6 This university has a very big campus – there are about twenty college buildings and several houses for students to live in.

7 It is very important to plan your day. Make sure there is time for college work and family life.

8 I watched the new Indian film at the cinema yesterday.

Presenter: **Lesson 2: Practising listening**

C Listen to Mrs Penn's definitions and check your answers.

Mrs Penn: **a** I'm going to give you your schedule – that's the days and times of your classes – for this semester, OK?

b First I want you to write the start time and the end time of each period – in other words, each part of the day.

c Lunch is served in the cafeteria – that's the restaurant on the campus.

d You have a short recess – I mean, a short break between classes.

Presenter: **D Mrs Penn is going to give you your schedule. Listen and answer these questions.**

Mrs Penn: OK. Is everybody ready? Have you all got a pencil? Good. I'm going to give you your schedule – that's the days and times of your classes – for this semester, OK? Can you fill it in as I read it out? If you're not sure about anything, ask your friends after this talk. OK. First I want you to write the start time and the end time of each period – in other words, each part of the day. As you can see, there are six periods, three in the morning and three in the afternoon. There's also a lunch period which lasts an hour. Lunch is served in the cafeteria – that's the restaurant on the campus. OK. Each period is one hour, so that's three hours in the morning and … how many hours in the afternoon?

Student 1: Three.

Mrs Penn: Good. The first period begins at 9 o'clock. So can you write 9 o'clock in the first morning space? When does the first period end?

Student 2: Half past nine.

Mrs Penn: No, not half past nine.

Student 3: 9.45?

Mrs Penn: No! Come on, think!

Student 1: 10 o'clock.

Mrs Penn: Why?

Student 1: Because each period is one hour.

Mrs Penn: Right. Good. So the next period begins at 10 o'clock, right?

Student 1: Yes.

Mrs Penn: Wrong. You have a short recess – I mean, a short break between classes. The recess is 10 minutes long. So the next period begins at …?

Student 2: Five past ten.

Student 3: Ten past ten.

Mrs Penn: That's right. OK. So now you can fill in the other times …

Presenter: **E Listen again.**
[REPEAT OF LESSON 2 EXERCISE D]

Presenter: **F 2 Listen and check your ideas.**

Voice:			
	a	each	column 2
	b	give	column 1
	c	mean	column 2
	d	read	column 2
	e	see	column 2
	f	six	column 1
	g	this	column 1
	h	three	column 2
	i	begins	column 1
	j	between	column 2

Presenter: **G 2 Listen and check your ideas.**

Voice:			
	a	about	letter b
	b	because	letter b
	c	begins	letter b
	d	pencil	letter p
	e	between	letter b
	f	break	letter b
	g	space	letter p
	h	campus	letter p
	i	part	letter p
	j	period	letter p

Presenter: **Lesson 3: Learning new listening skills**

B 1 Listen to eight times. Letter the clocks A to H.

Voice:		
	a	twenty to ten
	b	quarter past seven
	c	six o'clock
	d	twenty past four
	e	It's ten to four.
	f	ten past eight
	g	half past eleven
	h	quarter to three

Presenter: **3 Listen to the times again and check.**
[REPEAT OF LESSON 3 EXERCISE B1]

Presenter: **C 3 Listen and check your ideas.**

Mrs Penn:		
	a	Have you all got a pencil?
	b	ask your friends
	c	after this talk
	d	the start time
	e	each part of the day
	f	in the afternoon
	g	it lasts an hour
	h	in the cafeteria
	i	on the campus
	j	half past nine

Presenter: **Lesson 4: Applying new listening skills**

C Mrs Penn runs the extracurricular activities at Greenhill College. Listen and find out:

1 the meaning of extracurricular;

2 the extracurricular activities at the college – tick the activities on the notice board.

Mrs Penn: OK, so that's the schedule. Now, some other information for you. We have extracurricular activities – that means extra things you can do after college work – every evening, so can you make a note of these? If you want to do any of the activities, just come along to the first meeting this week. Right. First, we have Sports Club on Saturday at 8 o'clock in the evening – you can do basketball, handball, table tennis and lots of other sports.

Then there's Film Night on Sunday, starting at 8.30. We have a different film every week and after the film, there's a discussion.

It's Quiz Time on Monday. Come with a friend and take part in a General Knowledge quiz. That starts at quarter to eight.

Computer Club is on Tuesday. It doesn't matter whether you are a beginner or an expert. Come and learn or just have fun. Computer Club starts at quarter past eight.

Finally, we have Music Makers on Wednesday night. If you play an instrument or want to learn, join the music makers at half past seven. I'll run through those again in case you missed anything.

Presenter:	**D Listen again and write in the days and times for each activity that you ticked.** [REPEAT OF LESSON 4 EXERCISE C]
Presenter:	**Section 2: Speaking** **Lesson 1: Vocabulary for speaking** **B Listen and repeat the green words.**
Voice:	breakfast diary dinner last period second
Presenter:	**Lesson 2: Practising speaking** **B 2 Listen to Martino talking about his day. Fill in the missing times.**

Martino: It's Monday tomorrow. I've got a really busy day. From nine o'clock to eleven ten, I've got General Studies. Then I've got a free period – that's a period with no class – from eleven twenty to twelve twenty. I have to revise for a test in the afternoon. Lunch starts at twenty past twelve. It lasts an hour. Then I've got P.E. from twenty past one to twenty past two, followed by English from half past two to half past three. I've got another free period from twenty to four to twenty to five, then I'm playing handball with Peter from quarter to five to quarter past.

Presenter:	**D Listen again and check your answers.** [REPEAT OF LESSON 2 EXERCISE B2]
Presenter:	**Lesson 3: Learning new speaking skills** **A 2 Listen and check your order.**
Voice:	1 nine o'clock 2 ten ten 3 eleven fifteen 4 quarter to twelve 5 five past one 6 half past two 7 twenty to three 8 four forty-five
Presenter:	**Theme 3: Work and Business** **Section 1: Listening** **Lesson 1: Vocabulary for listening** **B Listen to some sentences with the green words. Then complete each sentence.**
Voice:	1 People don't like him at work. They can't rely on him. They never know if he will be late, or not come to work at all.

2 It is very important to have good colleagues to work with in a job.
3 That work isn't urgent. You can do it tomorrow.
4 Where are the papers for my next meeting? Are they in the file?
5 If you are paid every month, we call that money salary.
6 Some companies make products – real things like computers, televisions or cars.
7 Some companies give services – like banks, cleaning companies or car hire companies.

Presenter:	**Lesson 2: Practising listening** **B Gerald Gardiner is a management consultant. He is at Greenhill College today. He is talking to the first-year students about work. Listen to the first part of his talk.** **1 How many points does he make?** **2 Can you remember any of the points?**
Gerald Gardiner:	How do you get a good job when you leave college? You start thinking about it NOW! Change the way that you think about college. Think of college as a job – your job. You will find it much easier then to live in the world of work in two or three years' time. So college should be a job. But what is a job? What must you do in a job? I'm going to tell you nine things. Number 1: You must go to work every day. Number 2: You must be punctual – that means, you must always be on time. Number 3: You must respect your manager – the person who gives you orders – and your colleagues – that is, the people you work with. Number 4: You must also respect the customers, in other words, the people who buy things from the company. Number 5: You must do all the tasks or pieces of work that your manager gives you. Number 6: You must complete all your tasks on time. Number 7: You are responsible for the quality of your work – whether it is good or bad. Number 8: You must keep your workplace tidy – your desk, and any shelves or cupboards that you use. Number 9: You must organize your work files sensibly – in alphabetical order or chronologically – in other words, by date.
Presenter:	**C Listen again. How does he define these words? Match each word to a definition.** [REPEAT OF LESSON 2 EXERCISE B]
Presenter:	**E Listen again and check your answers.** [REPEAT OF LESSON 2 EXERCISE B]
Presenter:	**F 2 Listen and check your ideas.**
Voice:	are column D bad column C colleagues column B gives column A keep column B leave column D manager column C people column B pieces column B start column D that column C think column A

Presenter:	**G 2 Listen and check your ideas.**	
Voice:	a punctual	letter p
	b respect	letter p
	c buy	letter b
	d pieces	letter p
	e sensibly	letter b
	f people	letter p
	g job	letter b
	h company	letter p
	i responsible	letter p
	j workplace	letter p
	k complete	letter p
	l person	letter p

Presenter:	**Lesson 3: Learning new listening skills**
	B 2 Listen and check your ideas.

Voice:
a You must go to work every day.
b You must be punctual.
c You must respect your manager and your colleagues.
d You must also respect the customers.
e You must do all the tasks or pieces of work that your manager gives you.
f You must complete all your tasks on time.
g You are responsible for the quality of your work.
h You must keep your workplace tidy.
i You must organize your work files sensibly.

Presenter:	**C 2 Listen and check your answers.**	
Voice:	go	row A
	give	row A
	college	row B
	get	row A
	change	row B
	colleague	row A
	organize	row A

Presenter:	**4 Listen and check your answers.**	
Voice:	age	row B
	page	row B
	begin	row A
	charge	row B
	ago	row A
	again	row A
	large	row B
	big	row A

Presenter:	**6 Listen and check your answers.**	
Voice:	danger	row B
	angry	row A
	wage	row B
	magazine	row A
	rig	row A

Presenter:	**Lesson 4: Applying new listening skills**
	D 1 Listen and write one or two stressed words under Gerald's reasons in the blue table. Guess the spelling.

Gerald Gardiner: Why must you do all these things in a job? Let's look at each thing and suggest a reason.

You must go to work every day. Why? Because people rely on you. They need you to do your work so they can do their work.

You must be punctual. Why? Because people expect you at a certain time. If you are late, you waste their time.

You must respect your manager and your colleagues.

Why? Because you have to work together every day. You must respect the customers. Why? Because, in the end, they pay your wages.

You must do all the tasks that your manager gives you. Why? Because all jobs have interesting tasks and boring tasks, easy tasks and difficult tasks.

You must complete all your tasks on time. Why? Because other people need the information.

You are responsible for the quality of your work. Why? Because it is very bad for a company if a customer is dissatisfied with a product or service.

You must keep your workplace tidy. Why? Because it is rude to make other people put up with your mess.

You must organize your work files sensibly. Why? Because you might be ill one day. Then a manager or colleague will have to find urgent papers in your work files.

Presenter:	**2 Listen again. Are Gerald's reasons the same as yours? Listen for the important words.**
	[REPEAT OF LESSON 4 EXERCISE D]

Presenter:	**Section 2: Speaking**
	Lesson 1: Vocabulary for speaking
	B Listen and repeat the green words.
Voice:	assistant
	checkout
	clerk
	counsellor
	guide
	operator
	telesales

Presenter:	**Lesson 2: Practising speaking**
	C Julia's friend, Carla Fernandez, is talking to her. Listen.

Carla: Hi, Julia. What are you doing?
Julia: I'm using this web page to help me find a summer job. It says a good summer job for me is … nursery school assistant or shop assistant. I think that's a stupid suggestion! I don't like working with children and I don't like selling things.
Carla: Are you going to get a job in the college holidays?
Julia: I'd like to. What about you?
Carla: Yes, I think so.
Julia: What would you like to do?
Carla: I'm not sure.
Julia: OK. I'll ask you the questions and let's see what the computer suggests.
Carla: OK.
Julia: Question 1. Would you like to work in your own country or abroad?
Carla: What does it mean, abroad?
Julia: It means in another country – Greece or France, for example.
Carla: Oh, I'd like to work abroad.
Julia: Question 2. Do you like working alone or with other people?
Carla: With other people, definitely. I don't like working alone.
Julia: Question 3. Do you like working inside or outside?
Carla: Um, let me think. Inside. No, I'll change that. Outside.
Julia: OK. So I just click 'Find' and …
Carla: Why are you laughing?
Julia: It says … a good job for you is … a camp counsellor.
Carla: Well … I agree. I think that is a good suggestion.

Presenter:	**E**	**Listen to this part of the conversation again and check your answers.**
Carla:		Are you going to get a job in the college holidays?
Julia:		I'd like to. What about you?
Carla:		Yes, I think so.
Julia:		What would you like to do?
Carla:		I'm not sure.
Julia:		Would you like to work in your own country or abroad?
Carla:		Oh, I'd like to work abroad.
Julia:		Do you like working alone or with other people?
Carla:		With other people, definitely. I don't like working alone.
Julia:		Do you like working inside or outside?
Carla:		Um, let me think. Inside. No, I'll change that. Outside.

Presenter: Theme 4: Science and Nature
Section 1: Listening
Lesson 1: Vocabulary for listening
C Listen to a paragraph. Then write one of the green words in each space.

Voice: Science is the study of how things work in the world. A scientist usually works in a laboratory. He or she tests things to find out the facts. He or she often puts the facts in a table, with columns of information, or in a graph, with blocks or lines that represent the information.

Presenter: Lesson 2: Practising listening
C 1 Listen to the introduction to the programme. Tick each point in the programme information when Arthur mentions it.

Arthur Burns: This week on *So you want to be…* we are looking at the job of the scientist. What is science? What do scientists do? What is scientific method? And the most important question of all: Is science the right career for you?

Presenter: **2 Listen to the first part of the programme. Put your hand up when Arthur starts to talk about a new point.**

Arthur Burns: First, what is science? Science is the study of how things work in the world. The word science comes from Greek and Latin words meaning 'to know'. What do scientists do? Well, scientists are not satisfied just to think something is true. They must prove it. Proving means showing that something is always true. In this way, scientists are different from other people. Let me show you the difference.
I know that plants need sunlight and water to live. At least, I think that's true. But thinking is not enough for a scientist. If a scientist thinks something is true, he or she wants to prove it.
How can scientists prove that something is true? They must follow the scientific method. A method is a way of doing something. But what is the scientific method? It works like this: Firstly, a scientist makes a hypothesis, which means an idea of the truth. Then he or she tests the hypothesis. Scientists can test hypotheses in two main ways. They can do an experiment, which means a test in a laboratory. Scientists study what happens during the experiment. Or they can do research, which means looking up information. They usually do research in a library or, nowadays, on the Internet. With research, scientists look at what happened in the past.
In both cases – experiments and research – they collect

data. Data is information before it is organized. Then they display the results in a table or a graph. Then they draw conclusions. Conclusions are what you learn from an experiment. The hypothesis is proved – or disproved. Does this sound interesting to you? Is science the right career for you?

Presenter: **D Listen again. How does Arthur Burns define these words?**
[REPEAT OF LESSON 2 EXERCISE C2]

Presenter: **E Look at the student notes on the right. Listen to the first part of the programme again. Complete the notes by writing one word in each space.**
[REPEAT OF LESSON 2 EXERCISE C2]

Presenter: **F 2 Listen and check your ideas.**
Voice:	display	column A
	even	column B
	enough	column A
	graph	column D
	Greek	column B
	happen	column C
	if	column A
	lab	column C
	past	column D
	plant	column D

Presenter: **G 2 Listen and check your ideas.**
Voice:	a	prove	letter p
	b	display	letter p
	c	both	letter b
	d	table	letter b
	e	past	letter p
	f	disprove	letter p
	g	hypothesis	letter p
	h	experiment	letter p
	i	lab	letter b
	j	happen	letter p

Presenter: Lesson 3: Learning new listening skills
C 2 Listen to some of Arthur's sentences. Choose the next word from the yellow box each time Arthur pauses. Write the number beside the word.
Arthur Burns: 1 Science is the study of how things work in the [PAUSE] world.
2 The word 'science' comes from Greek and Latin words meaning to [PAUSE] know.
3 Scientists must prove that something is [PAUSE] true.
4 They must follow the scientific [PAUSE] method.
5 Scientists must collect [PAUSE] data.
6 They display the results in a table or [PAUSE] graph.

Presenter: **D 2 Listen and check your answers.**
Voice:	that	column B
	the	column B
	they	column B
	both	column A
	then	column B
	there	column B
	hypothesis	column A
	with	column B
	thing	column A
	truth	column A

Presenter:	**E 2 Listen and check your answers.**	
Voice:	test	
	when	
	then	
	pen	
	she	
	bed	
	many	
	any	
	head	
	again	

Presenter: Lesson 4: **Applying new listening skills**
B Listen to the next part of the programme with Arthur Burns. What does Arthur ask you to do? Make a sentence with these groups of words.

Arthur Burns: At the beginning of the programme, I said: I think plants need sunlight and water to live. But a scientist isn't satisfied with think. He or she wants to know. How can I prove that plants need sunlight and water to live? Can you think of an experiment to prove this hypothesis? I'll be back after these messages.

Presenter: **D Listen to the next part of the programme. When Arthur stops speaking, say the next word.**

Arthur Burns: Welcome back. Well, did you think of an [PAUSE] experiment?
If you did, perhaps a career in science is right for you.
If you didn't … well, perhaps you would like to hear about my [PAUSE] experiment.
Remember: my hypothesis was that plants need sunlight and water to live.
The experiment: I bought three plants of the same type.
I put each plant into a [PAUSE] pot. The pots were all the same size.
I filled each pot with the same kind of [PAUSE] soil.
I put each plant pot on a [PAUSE] saucer.
I put all three plants outside.
I covered Plant 1 with black plastic. So Plant 1 did not have any [PAUSE] sunlight.
I watered Plant 1 and Plant 3 for one week but I did not give Plant 2 any [PAUSE] water.
What result did I get?
Remember: Plant 1 did not have any sunlight.
It was yellow and very [PAUSE] small.
Plant 2 did not have any water.
It was [PAUSE] dead.
Plant 3 had sunlight and water.
It was green and very [PAUSE] healthy.
My conclusion is: Plants need sunlight and water to live.
I have proved my hypothesis.
Have I proved that science is a good career for you?

Presenter: Section 2: **Speaking**
Lesson 1: **Vocabulary for speaking**
B Listen and repeat the green words.

Voice: diagram
experiment
explain
explanation
natural
sunrise
sunset

Presenter: Lesson 2: **Practising speaking**
B Martha's friend, Ruth, comes into the cafe. Listen to the conversation. Which question can Ruth answer?

Ruth:	Hi, Martha. How are you?
Martha:	I'm fine, thanks. Have a seat.
Ruth:	Thanks. What are you doing?
Martha:	I'm thinking about this competition.
Ruth:	Oh, a competition. I like competitions.
Martha:	Could you help me, then?
Ruth:	Yes, of course. I'll give you a hand.
Martha:	Thanks. Do you know anything about science and nature?
Ruth:	You mean birds and weather and things?
Martha:	Yes, things like that.
Ruth:	Oh, no. Sorry. I'm afraid I don't.
Martha:	That's a pity. Neither do I.
Ruth:	Well, let's try, anyway. What are they asking?
Martha:	OK. This is the first one. Question A. Why is the sky blue?
Ruth:	Well, it's because … it's the colour of … it's … I have no idea.
Martha:	Oh. Question B. Why is the sky red at sunrise and sunset?
Ruth:	Ah, that's easier. It's red because … the red colour comes from … No, I don't know that one either. Do you know?
Martha:	No, I don't. OK. Question C. Why are the clouds white or grey?
Ruth:	I really don't know.
Martha:	Well, here's the last one. Why does it rain?
Ruth:	Oh, I know that one.
Martha:	You know this one?
Ruth:	Yes, I do.
Martha:	So what's the answer?

Presenter: **C 2 Listen again to the first part of the conversation and check your ideas.**

Ruth:	Hi, Martha. How are you?
Martha:	I'm fine, thanks. Have a seat.
Ruth:	Thanks. What are you doing?
Martha:	I'm thinking about this competition.
Ruth:	Oh, a competition. I like competitions.
Martha:	Could you help me, then?
Ruth:	Yes, of course. I'll give you a hand.
Martha:	Thanks. Do you know anything about science and nature?
Ruth:	You mean birds and weather and things?
Martha:	Yes, things like that.
Ruth:	Oh, no. Sorry. I'm afraid I don't.
Martha:	That's a pity. Neither do I.
Ruth:	Well, let's try, anyway. What are they asking?

Presenter: Theme 5: **The Physical World**
Section 1: **Listening**
Lesson 1: **Vocabulary for listening**
C Listen to descriptions of six countries. Look at the map. Find each country.

Voice:
1 It is in North America. It is north of the USA.
2 It is in Asia. It is southeast of Pakistan.
3 It is in Africa. It is west of Egypt.
4 It is in Europe. It is west of Spain.
5 It is in Australasia. It is a large island. It is on the Tropic of Capricorn. It is near New Zealand.
6 It is in South America. It is between the Equator and the Tropic of Capricorn. It is north of Argentina.

Presenter:	**Lesson 2: Practising listening**
	B 1 Listen. Donna pauses a few times in her questions. Guess the word she is going to say next on each occasion. Listen and check your ideas.
Donna:	Where are you [PAUSE] from, Fatma?
Fatma:	I'm from Kuwait.
Donna:	Where's [PAUSE] that?
Fatma:	It's in the north of the Gulf. It's northeast of Saudi Arabia.
Donna:	And where do you come [PAUSE] from in Kuwait?
Fatma:	I come from Al Khiran.
Donna:	How do you spell [PAUSE] that?
Fatma:	A-L K-H-I-R-A-N.
Donna:	Which part of the [PAUSE] country is that in?
Fatma:	Well, Kuwait is very small, but it's in the southeast.
Donna:	Is Al Khiran the capital?
Fatma:	No. The capital is Kuwait City.
Donna:	What about you, Fairuza?
Fairuza:	I'm from Oman.
Donna:	Is that in the Gulf, [PAUSE] too?
Fairuza:	Yes, well, not exactly. It's southeast of the UAE and Saudi Arabia.
Donna:	Does it have a long coastline?
Fairuza:	Yes, that's right. It has a coastline on the Arabian Sea.
Donna:	And what's your home [PAUSE] town?
Fairuza:	I'm from Salalah.
Donna:	Sorry. What did you [PAUSE] say?
Fairuza:	I said, Salalah.
Donna:	How do you spell [PAUSE] that?
Fairuza:	S-A-L-A-L-A-H.
Donna:	Is that the [PAUSE] capital?
Fairuza:	No, the capital is Muscat.
Donna:	Which part of the country is Salalah [PAUSE] in?
Fairuza:	It's in the south.

Presenter:	**B 3 Listen again. Complete the information about Kuwait and Oman.**
	[REPEAT OF LESSON 2 EXERCISE B1 WITHOUT PAUSES]

Presenter:	**D 2 Listen and check your ideas.**
Voice:	city — columns A and B
	did — column A
	east — column B
	exactly — columns A, C and B
	Oman — column D
	said — column E
	Salalah — column D
	spell — column E
	west — column E

Presenter:	**E 2 Listen and check your ideas.**
Voice:	a about — letter b
	b capital — letter p
	c north — letters t and h
	d part — letter p
	e south — letters t and h
	f spell — letter p

Presenter:	**F Listen and complete these words from earlier themes.**
Voice:	1 college
	2 display
	3 experiment
	4 job

5 manager
6 method
7 past
8 prove
9 think
10 punctual

Presenter:	**Lesson 3: Learning new listening skills**
	B 3 Listen and put the other letters of the alphabet into the correct column, according to the vowel sound.
Voice:	A B C D E F G H I J K L M N O P Q R S T U V W X Y Z

Presenter:	**C 1 Listen to the spellings on the cassette. Write the letters and find out the words.**
Voice:	1 U-K
	2 U-A-E
	3 U-S-A
	4 O-M-A-N
	5 Q-A-T-A-R
	6 K-U-W-A-I-T
	7 B-A-H-R-A-I-N
	8 Y-E-M-E-N
	9 J-A-P-A-N
	10 C-H-I-N-A
	11 S-A-U-D-I A-R-A-B-I-A
	12 G-U-L-F

Presenter:	**D 3 Listen and check your ideas.**
Voice:	it's
	is
	small
	south
	has
	east
	coast
	what's
	sorry
	does
	spell
	say
	towns

Presenter:	**E 4 Listen to the words in Exercises 1 and 2.**
Voice:	Exercise 1:
	on
	not
	from
	what
	come
	of
	sorry
	want
	was
	wash
	Exercise 2:
	for
	before
	more
	small
	talk
	war
	August
	taught
	north

Presenter: Lesson 4: Applying new listening skills
B 2 Listen and tick the topics you hear.

Lecturer: The Sultanate of Oman is situated north of the Equator. The capital city, Muscat, which in English is spelt M-U-S-C-A-T, is on the Tropic of Cancer – that's Tropic, T-R-O-P-I-C, of Cancer, C-A-N-C-E-R.
Oman is bordered to the northwest by the UAE and to the northeast by the Gulf of Oman.
To the west, there is a long, undefined border with Saudi Arabia, while to the southeast, Oman has a long coastline on the Arabian Sea.
In the southwest, there is a border with Yemen – Y-E-M-E-N.
There is also a small area in the far north that belongs to Oman. It is called Musandam – M-U-S-A-N-D-A-M. The total area of the country is 212,500 square kilometres. This is about three times the area of the UAE.
The country consists of stony desert, with a sandy desert in the southeast called Wahiba Sands – that's W-A-H-I-B-A. The border with Saudi Arabia is also sand desert. This is the famous Rub al Khali, or Empty Quarter.
There are mountains in the north of the country – they are called the Hajar – H-A-J-A-R. The highest point is Jebel Akhdar – J-E-B-E-L A-K-H-D-A-R.

Presenter: **3 Listen again and label the map.**
[REPEAT OF LESSON 4 EXERCISE B2]

Presenter: **Section 2: Speaking**
Lesson 1: Vocabulary for speaking
C Listen and repeat the green words.

Voice: Africa
America
Asia
continent
Europe
Oceania
the Middle East

Presenter: **Lesson 2: Practising speaking**
C 1 Listen to the conversation. Does Simon ask any of your questions from Exercises A or B?

Simon: Hi. My name's Simon. Simon Shepherd.
Zeki: Hello. I'm Zeki.
Simon: Can I help you?

Zeki: No, it's OK I can manage.
Simon: Are you going to the Geography lecture?
Zeki: Yes, I am. What about you?
Simon: Yes, me too. When does it start?
Zeki: Ten past ten, I think.
Simon: Where are you from, Zeki?
Zeki: I'm from Turkey.
Simon: Where's that?
Zeki: It's in Europe. It's north of Syria and Iraq.
Simon: And where do you come from in Turkey?
Zeki: I come from Mersin.
Simon: Sorry. What did you say?
Zeki: I said Mersin.
Simon: How do you spell that?
Zeki: M-E-R-S-I-N.
Simon: And how do you say it?
Zeki: Mersin.
Simon: Mersin. Which part of the country is that in?
Zeki: It's in the south.

Presenter: **C 2 Listen again. Complete the information about Zeki in the table.**
[REPEAT OF LESSON 2 EXERCISE C1]

D 2 Listen again and check your order.
[REPEAT OF LESSON 2 EXERCISE C1]

Presenter: **E 2 Listen and check your answers.**
Voice: a think in hi it's
The odd one out is hi.
b part what Iraq past
The odd one out is what.
c me help said spell
The odd one out is me.
d am about that manage
The odd one out is about.
e think north south that
The odd one out is that.

Presenter: **Lesson 4: Applying new speaking skills**
D 1 Read and listen to this short talk by Zeki about his country.

Zeki: My name is Zeki: Z-E-K-I. I am from Turkey, which is in Europe. Turkey is north of Syria and Iraq. It is south of Russia and Bulgaria. I come from a small town in Turkey called Mersin. That's M-E-R-S-I-N. It is in the south of the country.

Student A
Example:

One across and thirteen across – a person who teaches languages.

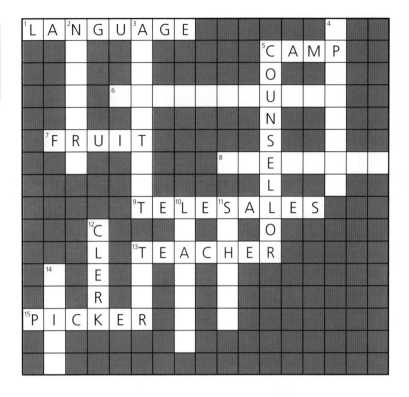

Student B
Example:

Two down, eleven down and three down – a person who helps in a school for young children.

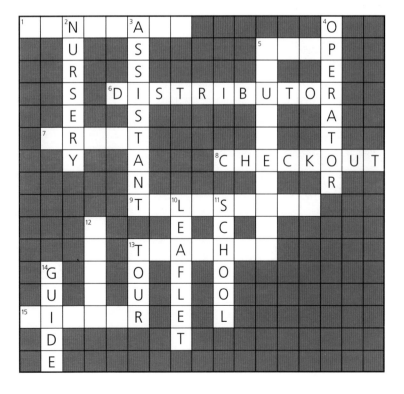

THEME 1
Education: Student Life

answer (n and v)
ask (v)
begin (v)
dictionary (n)
end (v)
explain (v)
history (n)
learn (v)
listen (v)
mathematics (n)
question (n)
read (v)
right (adj)
science (n)
spell (v)
student (n)
study (v)
teach (v)
test (n and v)
university (n)
write (v)
wrong (adj)
academic (adj)
advice (n)
advisor (n)
assignment (n)
college (n)
consider (v)
diploma (n)
draft (n)
faculty (n)
form (n)
head (n)
in charge (of) (adj)
instructor (n)
intelligence (n)
lecture (n)
literature (n)
meeting (n)
polite (adj)
principal (n)
relax (v)
respect (n and v)

responsible (for) (adj)
semester (n)
speech (n)
studies (n)
subject (n)
term (n)
year (n)

Words of your own:

_____
_____
_____
_____
_____
_____
_____
_____
_____
_____
_____
_____
_____
_____
_____
_____
_____
_____
_____
_____
_____
_____
_____
_____
_____

THEME 2
Daily Life: Organizing Your Time

afternoon (n)
autumn (n)
day (n)
evening (n)
first (adj)
hour (n)
last (adj)
late (adj)
later (adj)
midnight (n)
minute (n)
month (n)
morning (n)
night (n)
noon (n)
now (adv)
o'clock (adv)
past (n and adv)
quarter (n)
spring (n)
summer (n)
time (n)
today (n)
tomorrow (n)
tonight (n)
week (n)
winter (n)
year (n)
yesterday (n)
always (adv)
break (n)
breakfast (n)
campus (n)
chess (n)
club (n)
diary (n)
dinner (n)
film (n)
last (v)
music (n)
never (adv)
often (adv)
once (adv)

on time (prep)
period (n)
plan (v)
regular (adj)
regularly (adv)
restaurant (n)
schedule (n)
second (n)
social (adv)
social life (n)
sometimes (adv)
spend (v)
sports (n)
twice (adv)
usually (adv)
weekend (n)
weekly (adv)

Words of your own:

_____
_____
_____
_____
_____
_____
_____
_____
_____
_____
_____
_____
_____
_____
_____
_____
_____
_____

THEME 3
Work and Business: Work Starts Now!

company (n)
computer (n)
desk (n)
e-mail (n)
envelope (n)
factory (n)
file (n)
job (n)
letter (n)
manager (n)
office (n)
secretary (n)
shelf/shelves (n)
shop (n)
start (v)
supermarket (n)
typist (n)
website (n)
work (n and v)
working hours (n)
applicant (n)
assist (v)
assistant (n)
benefit (n)
career (n)
checkout (n)
clerk (n)
colleague (n)
counsellor (n)
employ (v)
employable (adj)
employee (n)
employer (n)
employment (n)
experience (n)
guide (n)
operator (n)
overtime (n)
papers (n)
product (n)
qualification (n)
rely on (v)
requirement (n)

salary (n)
service (n)
telesales (n)
urgent (adj)

Words of your own:

_____
_____
_____
_____
_____
_____
_____
_____
_____
_____
_____
_____
_____
_____
_____
_____
_____
_____
_____
_____
_____
_____
_____
_____
_____
_____
_____
_____
_____

THEME 4
Science and Nature: The Sun, The Air, The Rain

black (adj)
blue (adj)
brown (adj)
cloud (n)
cold (adj)
colour (n and v)
dry (adj)
flower (n)
fog (n)
forest (n)
grass (n)
green (adj)
grey (adj)
hot (adj)
island (n)
lake (n)
mountain (n)
orange (adj)
rain (n and v)
red (adj)
river (n)
sea (n)
sky (n)
snow (n and v)
sun (n)
temperature (n)
thunderstorm (n)
tree (n)
water (n)
weather (n)
wet (adj)
white (adj)
wind (n)
yellow (adj)
average (adj)
column (n)
decrease (n)
diagram (n)
experiment (n)
explain (v)
explanation (n)
graph (n)
increase (n)

laboratory (n)
large (adj)
latitude (n)
longitude (n)
meridian (n)
natural (adj)
pole (n)
row (n)
science (n)
scientific (adj)
scientist (n)
small (adj)
source (n)
steady (adj)
sunrise (n)
sunset (n)
table (n)
test (v)
the Earth (n)
the Equator (n)
unit of measurement (n)

Words of your own:

_____
_____
_____
_____
_____
_____
_____
_____
_____
_____
_____
_____
_____
_____
_____
_____
_____
_____
_____
_____

THEME 5
The Physical World: Where Is Your Country?

behind *(prep)*
between *(prep)*
corner *(n)*
country *(n)*
east *(n)*
in front of *(prep)*
in the centre of *(prep)*
island *(n)*
lake *(n)*
left *(n)*
mountain *(n)*
near *(prep)*
next to *(prep)*
north *(n)*
opposite *(prep)*
right *(n)*
river *(n)*
sea *(n)*
south *(n)*
thank *(v)*
thank you *(interj)*
town *(n)*
west *(n)*
woman *(n)*
Africa *(n)*
America *(n)*
Asia *(n)*
border *(n and v)*
celebrate *(v)*
celebration *(n)*
ceremony *(n)*
compass *(n)*
continent *(n)*
Europe *(n)*
event *(n)*
festival *(n)*
landscape *(n)*
latitude *(n)*
locate *(v)*
location *(n)*
longitude *(n)*
Oceania *(n)*
region *(n)*

special *(adj)*
take place *(v)*
the Equator *(n)*
the Middle East *(n)*
the Tropic of Cancer *(n)*
the Tropic of Capricorn *(n)*
traditional *(adj)*

Words of your own:

_____
_____
_____
_____
_____
_____
_____
_____
_____
_____
_____
_____
_____
_____
_____
_____
_____
_____
_____
_____
_____
_____

academic *(adj)*
advice *(n)*
advisor *(n)*
Africa *(n)*
afternoon *(n)*
always *(adv)*
America *(n)*
answer *(n and v)*
applicant *(n)*
Asia *(n)*
ask *(v)*
assignment *(n)*
assist *(v)*
assistant *(n)*
autumn *(n)*
average *(adj)*
begin *(v)*
behind *(prep)*
benefit *(n)*
between *(prep)*
black *(adj)*
blue *(adj)*
border *(n and v)*
break *(n)*
breakfast *(n)*
brown *(adj)*
campus *(n)*
career *(n)*
celebrate *(v)*
celebration *(n)*
ceremony *(n)*
checkout *(n)*
chess *(n)*
clerk *(n)*
cloud *(n)*
club *(n)*
cold *(adj)*
colleague *(n)*
college *(n)*
colour *(n and v)*
column *(n)*
company *(n)*
compass *(n)*
computer *(n)*
consider *(v)*
continent *(n)*
corner *(n)*

counsellor *(n)*
country *(n)*
day *(n)*
decrease *(n)*
desk *(n)*
diagram *(n)*
diary *(n)*
dictionary *(n)*
dinner *(n)*
diploma *(n)*
draft *(n)*
dry *(adj)*
east *(n)*
e-mail *(n)*
employ *(v)*
employable *(adj)*
employee *(n)*
employer *(n)*
employment *(n)*
end *(v)*
envelope *(n)*
Europe *(n)*
evening *(n)*
event *(n)*
experience *(n)*
experiment *(n)*
explain *(v)*
explanation *(n)*
factory *(n)*
faculty *(n)*
festival *(n)*
file *(n)*
film *(n)*
first *(adj)*
flower *(n)*
fog *(n)*
forest *(n)*
form *(n)*
graph *(n)*
grass *(n)*
green *(adj)*
grey *(adj)*
guide *(n)*
head *(n)*
history *(n)*
hot *(adj)*
hour *(n)*

in charge (of) (adj)
in front of (prep)
in the centre of (prep)
increase (n)
instructor (n)
intelligence (n)
island (n)
job (n)
laboratory (n)
lake (n)
landscape (n)
large (adj)
last (v and adj)
late (adj)
later (adj)
latitude (n)
learn (v)
lecture (n)
left (n)
letter (n)
listen (v)
literature (n)
locate (v)
location (n)
longitude (n)
manager (n)
mathematics (n)
meeting (n)
meridian (n)
midnight (n)
minute (n)
month (n)
morning (n)
mountain (n)
music (n)
natural (adj)
near (prep)
never (adv)
next to (prep)
night (n)
noon (n)
north (n)
now (adv)
o'clock (adv)
Oceania (n)
office (n)

often (adv)
once (adv)
on time (prep)
operator (n)
opposite (prep)
orange (adj)
overtime (n)
papers (n)
past (n and adv)
period (n)
plan (v)
pole (n)
polite (adj)
principal (n)
product (n)
qualification (n)
quarter (n)
question (n)
rain (n and v)
read (v)
red (adj)
region (n)
regular (adj)
regularly (adv)
relax (v)
rely on (v)
requirement (n)
respect (n and v)
responsible (for) (adj)
restaurant (n)
right (adj and n)
river (n)
row (n)
salary (n)
schedule (n)
science (n)
science (n)
scientific (adj)
scientist (n)
sea (n)
second (n)
secretary (n)
semester (n)
service (n)
shelf/shelves (n)
shop (n)

sky (n)
small (adj)
snow (n and v)
social (adv)
social life (n)
sometimes (adv)
source (n)
south (n)
special (adj)
speech (n)
spell (v)
spend (v)
sports (n)
spring (n)
start (v)
steady (adj)
student (n)
studies (n)
study (v)
subject (n)
summer (n)
sun (n)
sunrise (n)
sunset (n)
supermarket (n)
table (n)
take place (v)
teach (v)
telesales (n)
temperature (n)
term (n)
test (n and v)
thank (v)
thank you (interj)
the Earth (n)
the Equator (n)
the Middle East (n)
the Tropic of Cancer (n)
the Tropic of Capricorn (n)
thunderstorm (n)
time (n)
today (n)
tomorrow (n)
tonight (n)
town (n)

traditional (adj)
tree (n)
twice (adv)
typist (n)
unit of measurement (n)
university (n)
urgent (adj)
usually (adv)
water (n)
weather (n)
website (n)
week (n)
weekend (n)
weekly (adv)
west (n)
wet (adj)
white (adj)
wind (n)
winter (n)
woman (n)
work (n and v)
working hours (n)
write (v)
wrong (adj)
year (n)
yellow (adj)
yesterday (n)